Amazing You!

GETTING SMART ABOUT YOUR PRIVATE PARTS

by **Dr. Gail Saltz**
illustrated by **Lynne Cravath**

DUTTON CHILDREN'S BOOKS ◉ NEW YORK

To Emily, Kimberly, and Victoria,
who always ask the best questions
G.S.

DUTTON CHILDREN'S BOOKS
A division of Penguin Young Readers Group

Published by the Penguin Group
Penguin Group (USA) Inc., 375 Hudson Street, New York, New York 10014, U.S.A.
Penguin Group (Canada), 90 Eglinton Avenue East, Suite 700, Toronto, Ontario, Canada M4P 2Y3 (a division of Pearson Penguin Canada Inc.)
Penguin Books Ltd, 80 Strand, London WC2R 0RL, England
Penguin Ireland, 25 St Stephen's Green, Dublin 2, Ireland (a division of Penguin Books Ltd)
Penguin Group (Australia), 250 Camberwell Road, Camberwell, Victoria 3124, Australia (a division of Pearson Australia Group Pty Ltd)
Penguin Books India Pvt Ltd, 11 Community Centre, Panchsheel Park, New Delhi - 110 017, India
Penguin Group (NZ), Cnr Airborne and Rosedale Roads, Albany, Auckland 1310, New Zealand (a division of Pearson New Zealand Ltd)
Penguin Books (South Africa) (Pty) Ltd, 24 Sturdee Avenue, Rosebank, Johannesburg 2196, South Africa
Penguin Books Ltd, Registered Offices: 80 Strand, London WC2R 0RL, England

Text copyright © 2005 Gail Saltz, M.D.   Illustrations copyright © 2005 Lynne Cravath

CIP Data is available.

Published in the United States by Dutton Children's Books,
a division of Penguin Young Readers Group
345 Hudson Street, New York, New York 10014
www.penguin.com/youngreaders

Designed by Irene Vandervoort

Manufactured in China   First Edition

ISBN 978-0-525-47389-3

16 17 18 19 20

A NOTE TO PARENTS

If you're like most parents, you may find that your preschool child is beginning to ask questions about his or her body. Hopefully, this book will be a useful tool to guide you through those first conversations about sexuality.

Take a good look at
yourself in the mirror.

What do you see?

Head,
arms,
hands,
legs,
and feet?

Those are the parts of your body that we can *all* see. You use them every time you hug your mom, ride a bicycle, or eat a snack.

But what about the other parts, the parts that nobody else but you sees?

What

can

they

do?

We call those parts "private parts" because they stay hidden under your clothes or underwear. They belong to you, and they are special.

Do you have a funny name for your private parts?

pee-pee

tee-hee-hee!

weenie!

hot dog!

Something no one else but you knows about?

What is it?

Lots of people have their own special names for their private parts, but it's a good idea to know what the real names are, too.

If you're a girl, you have many private parts—some you can see and some you can't. Your vagina is an opening that is covered by two folds of skin, called labia. It's not the same opening that you use to urinate—that's called the urethra.

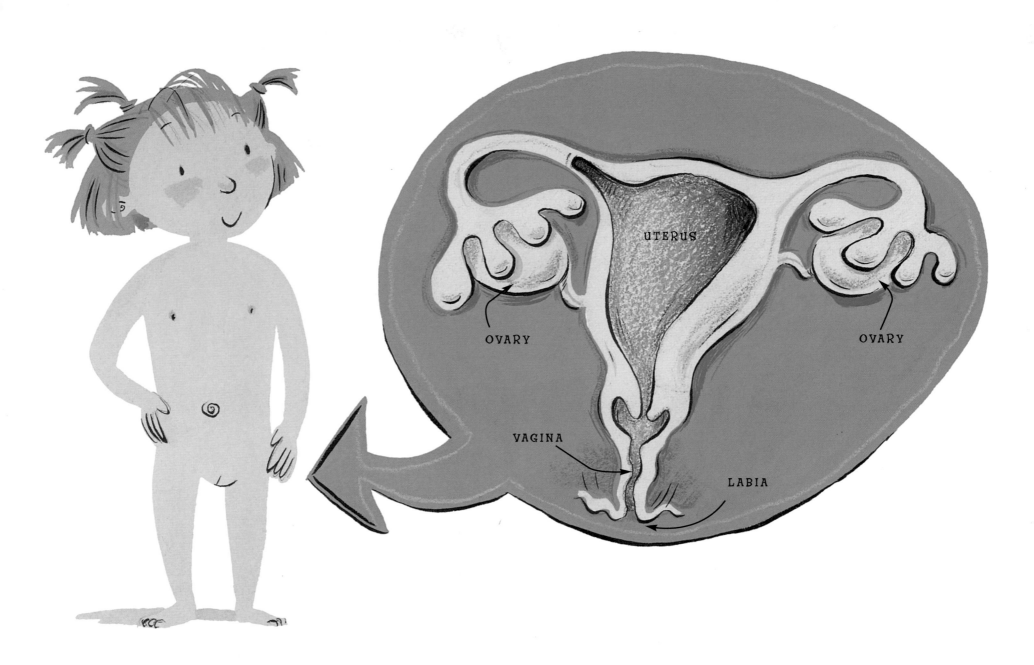

Here is a picture of some of your parts,
even those you can't see!

If you are a boy, you have a penis and a round sac, called the scrotum. You use your penis to urinate. It has a small hole in it, called the urethra, where the urine comes out.

Inside the sac under your penis are soft balls called testicles. Someday, when you're a grown-up, your testicles will begin to make sperm. Sperm look sort of like tadpoles, with a tail that helps them swim.

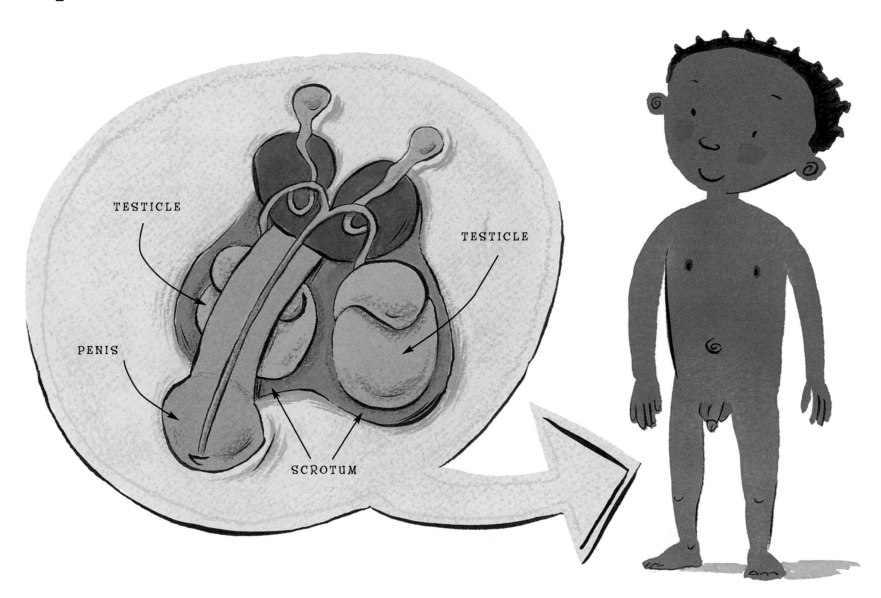

It's perfectly natural to be curious about your private parts and to want to touch them. But this is something you should do only in a private place, like your room.

Your body is growing and changing every day,
and your private parts are growing and changing, too.

Wheeee!

Here I go! Out I'm going!

EGG

EGGS

EGGS

OVARY

If you are a girl, your whole body will grow, including your vagina. One day, when you are much older, your ovaries inside your body will begin to release tiny eggs—even tinier than the dot at the bottom of this exclamation point!

If you are a boy, your penis and testicles will grow as your body gets bigger. Your testicles will begin to make sperm.

TESTICLE

SPERM

SPERM

It's crowded in here!

When a man and a woman love each other and decide
that they want to have a baby, a man's sperm joins with
a woman's egg. From the egg and sperm, a baby will grow.

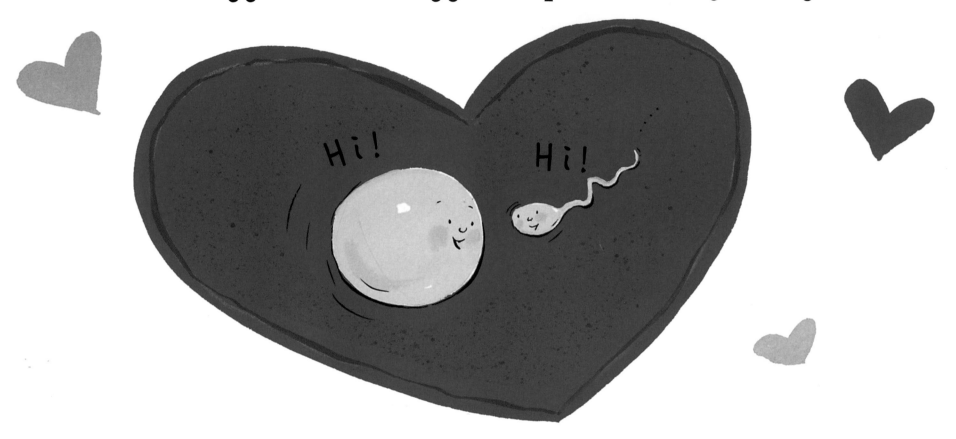

The baby grows inside the mother's uterus, a nice warm space
below the stomach. The baby gets all its food and air from a tube
called the umbilical cord, which attaches the baby to its mother.
When all the baby's body parts are grown and ready, then it will
be born. This takes about nine months.

When the baby is ready to come out, the mother's uterus will start to squeeze, and little by little it will squeeze the baby out.

The baby will come out of the mother's vagina, which
is very, very stretchy. It stretches wide enough for the baby
to come out and then goes back to the way it was before.

Then the baby will go home to be cuddled and
loved and grow into a child ... just like you did.

You can feel proud of your body. The smarter you are about your private parts, the better you'll feel about yourself.

So take another look at yourself in the mirror.

What
do
you
see?

Amazing you!

AUTHOR'S NOTE

Sexual curiosity starts at a very young age, so it's perfectly normal for your children to be interested in their private parts. It's normal for them to ask you questions, too. If you feel awkward having these first conversations about sexuality, remember you're not alone. The key is to be open and honest. When your child begins to ask questions, take the opportunity to establish yourself as the primary source of information about sex.

As parents, we pass along many things to our children, including our sexual attitudes. It's up to us to set the stage for their sexual life, which means helping them to not feel ashamed of their own bodies. If you harbor feelings that sex is dirty and shameful, then you may unwittingly pass this on to your child. You may also convey a sense of shame when you avoid giving any name to your child's genitals. References to "down there" and "that place" imply that it's too embarrassing to even mention one's private parts.

In order for our children to have pride in their genitals, we have to view them positively ourselves. It's best to use universal terms that are anatomical, such as *vagina, labia, penis,* and *testicles*. If you are unsure of the anatomical terms, get familiar with them so that you can explain them to your children when they ask.

Do not panic if your child masturbates; it's perfectly normal. It's best to encourage him or her to do it in a private place. If, however, your child is constantly masturbating, it could be a sign that he or she is feeling overwhelmingly anxious about something. If you have concerns about your child's masturbation, you should seek help from a professional.

Help your children to feel pleased with their bodies, but also tell them that no one else should ever be touching them. They have the right to say "No!" because they have ownership of their bodies.

Preschool children (ages one to six) will notice pregnant women and want to know where babies come from. Most are not ready to hear about intercourse and do not need to know about it yet. What they want to know is where in your body the baby grows and how it comes out. Do not make up stories involving storks or other magical events. Be honest with your children—it ruins the trust if you make up a story that you later have to correct. On the other hand, give them only the amount of information they can understand, depending on their age and maturity. An explanation of Dad's sperm joining Mom's egg is generally sufficient to help children understand how a baby begins to grow.

I hope that this book gives you a comfortable platform for further discussions with your children. Believe me, they will keep asking questions! The more you know about your child, the better prepared you will be to answer those questions and to help guide your child through all the exciting changes that are to come.